JACKIE
JOYNER-KERSEE

(Photo on font cover.)

Joyner-Kersee sets a new world record in the heptathlon.

(Photo on previous pages.)

Joyner-Kersee fails to clear the bar on this high jump attempt.

Text copyright © 1997 by The Child's World, Inc.
All rights reserved. No part of this book may be reproduced
or utilized in any form or by any means without written
permission from the Publisher.
Printed in the United States of America.

Photography supplied by Wide World Photos Inc.

Library of Congress Catalog-in-Publication Data
Rambeck, Richard
Jackie Joyner-Kersee / Richard Rambeck
p. cm.
Summary: An overview of the athletic accomplishments of the
track star who has been called the "first lady of the heptathlon."
ISBN 1-56766-271-4 (Lib. Bdg.)

1. Joyner-Kersee, Jacqueline, 1962 — Juvenile literature.
2. Track and field athletes — United States — Biography —
Juvenile literature. 3. Women track and field athletes — United
Statea — Biography — Juvenile liturature, [1. Joyner-Kersee,
Jacqueline, 1962. 2. Track and field athletes. 3. Afro-Americans —
Biography. 4. Women — Biography.]
I. Title
GV697.J69R68   1997   95-47112
796.42'092 — dc20   CIP
[B]   AC

JACKIE
JOYNER-KERSEE

BY RICHARD RAMBECK

THE CHILD'S WORLD

Jackie Joyner-Kersee didn't feel well at all. Her asthma was acting up, and she had a fever. Almost anyone else who felt that sick would have been in bed. Joyner-Kersee wasn't in bed, though. Instead, she was at the 1993 World Track Championships in Germany, competing in the seven-event heptathlon. Joyner-Kersee was in second place going into the final event. Sabine Braun, a German favorite of the home crowd, was leading by seven points.

German flags waved in the stands as Joyner-Kersee and Braun got ready for the last event, the 800 meters. "Sabine, Sabine, Sabine," the huge crowd chanted. Jackie Joyner-Kersee responded by starting her own, private chant. "Jackie, Jackie, Jackie," she said to herself. The race began, and Joyner-Kersee forgot all about how sick she was. She beat Braun by enough to overcome the German's seven-point lead. Joyner-Kersee, who hadn't lost a heptathlon since 1984, had won again.

"I wasn't afraid to run," she said after the race. "I was afraid I might die." She was kidding, but it was remarkable that she was able to do so well while feeling so poorly. "I definitely believe this is my greatest triumph," she said. Jackie Joyner-Kersee has had a lot of great triumphs. Some experts believe she is the

Joyner-Kersee and her Olympic gold medal in the 1992 heptathlon.

8

finest all-around woman athlete of all time. In Olympic competition, she has won three gold medals, one silver, and one bronze.

J oyner-Kersee is certainly one of the best ever in the heptathlon. This women's competition takes two days to complete its seven events. The heptathlon is scored on a point system. The better an athlete does in an event, the higher her score. To win a heptathlon, you must be able to run fast and for a long distance. You must have great jumping ability. And you must be strong. Quite simply, you must be an incredible all-around athlete.

The seven events in the heptathlon are the 110-meter hurdles, the shot put, the 200-meter dash, the long jump, the javelin throw, the high jump, and the 800 meters. From 1984 to 1994, Joyner-Kersee never lost a heptathlon competition. Instead, she won two Olympic gold medals, four world titles, and three Goodwill Games championships in the event. In 1986, she became the first woman ever to score 7,000 points in the heptathlon.

Less than a month after she set a world heptathlon record of 7,148 points, she broke her own record. Two years later, she set a new record when she won the 1988 Olympic gold medal.

Joyner-Kersee strides over a hurdle.

Joyner-Kersee shows off her second gold medal won at the 1988 Summer Olympics.

In fact, Joyner-Kersee has broken the world record in the heptathlon a total of four times! It's not her only event, though. She is also one of the best long-jumpers in the world. In fact, she won the Olympic gold medal in 1988 and the bronze in 1992 in that event.

Jackie Joyner-Kersee has become what could be called the first lady of the heptathlon. In fact, she was actually named after a First Lady. When she was born on March 3, 1962, her grandmother Evelyn Joyner suggested naming her after Jackie Kennedy. Jackie Kennedy was the wife of President John F. Kennedy, and the nation's First Lady. Why was Joyner-Kersee named after Jackie Kennedy? The answer came from Evelyn Joyner.

"Someday," said Evelyn Joyner, looking at the newborn baby, "this girl will be the first lady of something." Evelyn Joyner was a wise woman. Young Jackie grew up with a brother and two sisters in the Joyner family home in East St. Louis, Illinois. Her parents, Alfred and Mary, ran a strict household. "My mother, she was always telling us: Get an education. Be independent," Joyner-Kersee says. School came first; athletics came second.

Joyner-Kersee makes a big effort in the shotput.

16

There was a lot of athletic talent in the family. Jackie's brother, Al, who is two years older, won the 1984 Olympic gold medal in the long jump. Jackie's own track career began at age nine. She joined a track team, but was hardly an instant success. In her first race, she finished last. She wasn't discouraged, though. "I didn't have to win," she says about that first race. "I just wanted to get better." She did.

At age 14, Jackie decided she wanted to be an Olympic athlete. She watched the 1976 Olympics on television and became a big fan of U.S. sprinter Evelyn Ashford. She vowed to be just like

Ashford. Jackie even decided she wanted to attend the same university—UCLA. "She knew what she wanted to be, and she always kept moving in that direction," says Nino Fenney, Jackie's high school track coach. Jackie Joyner wound up getting a basketball scholarship to UCLA.

J oyner played basketball and volleyball and ran track at UCLA, but she was really a track person at heart. After graduating, she competed in the heptathlon in the 1984 Olympics. She finished second, only five points behind the winner. The competition was very close. If Joyner had long-jumped three centimeters farther, or run the 800 meters

Joyner-Kersee long jumps 23 feet on this attempt.

0.33 seconds faster, she would have won. It was a heartbreaking defeat, but Joyner never felt sorry for herself.

J oyner and her coach, Bob Kersee, set about trying to make her the best female athlete in the world. They worked together constantly, with Kersee pushing Joyner to improve every day. Soon, the two became more than track star and coach. They fell in love and were married in 1986, and she became known as Jackie Joyner-Kersee. Jackie and Bob have one track goal left. They want her to win the heptathlon at the 1996 Olympics in Atlanta. It would be a fitting end to a great career.